JOKES FOR KIDS

What's the best thing about elevator jokes?

They work on so
many levels.

What did the dog say
to the sandpaper?

Ruff!

Why did the dinosaur cross the road?

Because the chicken
wasn't born yet.

What do you call two birds in love?

Tweet-hearts.

Why was the man mad at the clock?

He was ticked off!

What animal always goes to bed with its shoes on?

A horse.

What did one wall say to the other wall?

I'll meet you at the corner.

What kind of music do mummies listen to?

Wrap music.

What do you call a bear with no ear?

A "B."

How do you keep
someone in suspense?

I'll tell you tomorrow.

Knock, knock.
Who's there? Wet.
Wet who?
Wet me in, it's
raining out here!

What do you call a story about a broken pencil?

Pointless.

What do chickens grow on?

Eggplants.

What did one eye say to the other?

Between you and me,
something smells.

What should you wear to a tea party?

A T-shirt.

Why did the banana go to the doctor?

Because it wasn't peeling well.

Where does a rat go when it has a toothache?

To the rodentist.

What does a nosey pepper do?

It gets jalapeño business!

What has two legs but can't walk?

A pair of pants.

Why did the frog take the bus to work today?

His car got toad away.

What musical instrument is found in the bathroom?

A tuba toothpaste.

Why did the kid run to school?

Because he was chased
by the spelling bee.

Why are fish so smart?

Because they are
always in a school.

What do you call two witches that live together?

Broom mates.

What is fast, loud, and crunchy?

A rocket chip.

Why don't traffic lights ever go swimming?

They take too long
to change.

Why did the surfer think the sea was his friend?

It gave him a big wave.

What kind of
monkey can fly?

A hot-air baboon.

What building in New York City has the most stories?

The public library.

What goes up and down but does not move?

Stairs.

Where do people learn to make ice cream?

In sundae school.

Why can't skeletons
play music?

They have no organs.

What do you get when you cross a fly, a car, and a dog?

A flying carpet.

What kind of fish goes great with peanut butter?

Jellyfish!

How was the snow globe feeling?

A little shaken.

What did Delaware?

A New Jersey.

What do you call an elephant that doesn't matter?

Irrelephant.

What bird loves construction work?

A crane.

Can February March?

No, but April May.

What kind of tree fits in your hand?

A palm tree.

I used to hate
body hair. . . but
it grew on me.

Why can't Monday lift Saturday?

It's a week day.

What do you call a fly with no wings?

A walk.

Why was the girl staring at the juice box?

It said "Concentrate."

Why was the computer late to work?

He had a hard drive.

Why are zombies
so good at tests?

They eat a lot of
brain food.

What did the apple tree say to the farmer?

Stop picking on me!

What's easy to get into, but hard to get out of?

Trouble.

What do you call a seagull that flies over the bay?

A bagel.

Why can't a bicycle
stand up?

It's two tired.

What do you call a boy named Lee that no one talks to?

Lonely.

How do you get straight A's?

Use a ruler.

How do you make
a tissue dance?

Put a little boogie in it.

Why don't scientists
trust atoms?

They make up everything.

What do you call a crazy spaceman?

An astronut.

What gets wetter
as it dries?

A towel.

What is a balloon's least favorite kind of music?

Pop.

How do snails fight?

They slug it out.

What do you call two spiders who just got married?

Newlywebs.

What do you call someone else's cheese?

Nacho cheese!

How do you know when the moon has had enough to eat?

It's full.

Why are ghosts such bad liars?

You can see right through them.

What did the buffalo say when his son left for school?

"Bison!!"

**What starts with a
P and ends with an
E and has thousands
of letters?**

The post office.

What is the math teacher's favorite dessert?

Pi.

Where do milk shakes come from?

Nervous cows.

What kind of place should you never take a dog?

A flea market.

What happened when the lion ate the comedian?

He felt a little funny.

What did the lunch box say to the banana?

You really have appeal.

Why did the cucumber call 911?

It was in a pickle.

Why don't crabs share their food?

They're shellfish.

Why don't honest people need beds?

They never lie.

Why did the square and triangle go to the gym?

To stay in shape.

How do you organize a space-themed party?

You planet.

What do you call a
bear with no teeth?

A gummy bear.

What do you call an elephant at the North Pole?

Lost.

Where are cars most likely to get flat tires?

At forks in the road.

How did Benjamin Franklin feel when he discovered electricity?

He was shocked.

What did the creek
say to the brook?

Stop babbling!

When is your door
not actually a door?

When it's actually ajar.

How do you stop an astronaut's baby from crying?

You rocket.

Why did the fox
cross the road?

To look for the chicken.

Which school
supply is king?

The ruler.

What does the toast wear to bed?

Jammies.

What did zero say to eight?

Nice belt.

What does a cow grow on its face?

A mooooostache.

What do you call a can opener that doesn't work?

A can't opener.

How do they answer the phone at the paint store?

Yellow?

Who can hold up a bus with one hand?

A crossing guard.

What do you call a funny mountain?

Hill-arious.

What did one toilet say to the other?

You look flushed.

What can fill up the room but takes no space?

Light.

What did the lawyer name his daughter?

Sue.

How does a cucumber becomes a pickle?

It goes through a jarring experience.

What did one plate say to the other plate?

Dinner is on me.

What do you call
a fake noodle?

An impasta.

What do you call
a tired pea?

Sleep pea.

What has six eyes but cannot see?

Three blind mice.

What do birds do on Halloween?

They go trick or tweeting.

Why did the star go to the bathroom?

It had to twinkle.

What do you give an angry alien?

Some space.

Add Your Own Jokes!

Printed in the USA
CPSIA information can be obtained
at www.ICGtesting.com
CBHW050925041024
15168CB00009B/107